Conservative vs. Liberal Ideologies and Applied Economics

Social Wealth and the Poverty of Tyranny

Volume 1

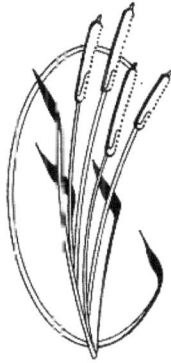

Conservative vs. Liberal Ideologies and Applied Economics

Social Wealth and the Poverty of Tyranny

Volume 1

by Bob Beadles

Editor
Jonathan Patterson

Cover Art & Graphics Designer
Brendan Rafko-Roberts

Senior Publisher
Steven Hill

ASA Publishing Corporation
ASA Publishing Company

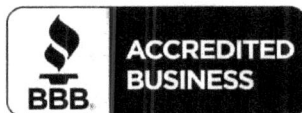

A Publisher Trademark Title page

ASA Publishing Corporation
An Accredited Publishing House with the BBB

105 E. Front St., Suite 101
Monroe, Michigan 48161
www.asapublishingcorporation.com

Copyrights©2015 Bob Beadles, All Rights Reserved
Book: Conservative vs. Liberal Ideologies and Applied Economics   *Volume 1*
Date Published: 08.23.15/Edition 1 *Trade Paperback*
Book ASAPCID: 2380673
ISBN: 978-1-886528-25-3
Library of Congress Cataloging-in-Publication Data

This book was published in the United States of America.
State of Michigan

Table of Contents

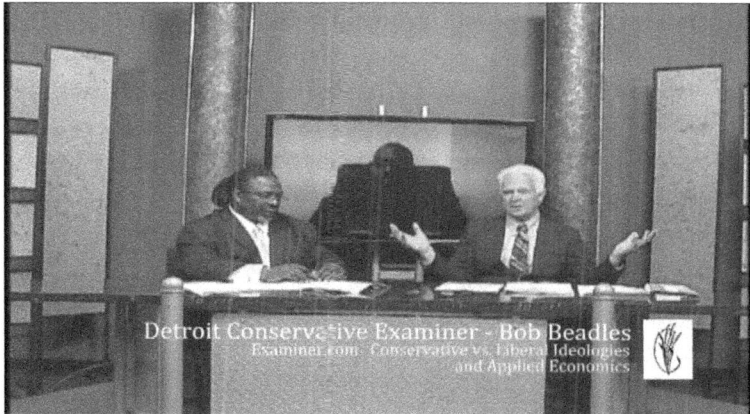

Detroit Conservative Examiner - Bob Beadles
Examiner.com Conservative vs. Liberal Ideologies
and Applied Economics

About the Political Analyst

Bob Beadles was born in Monroe, Michigan where he attended St. John the Baptist grade school and Monroe Catholic Central High School. He received a Bachelor of Science degree in economics from the University of Maryland.

The writer ran for the office of Michigan's 56th District Representative. As a District Representative, Bob's focus was to bring full employment to Michigan and especially Monroe.

Bob Beadles believes first and foremost in freedom. He often quotes George Washington who said: "Government is not reason, it is not eloquence; it is force. Like fire, it is a troublesome servant and a fearful master". That quote is used to emphasize the need for small and limited government.

He is also fond of quoting Lord Acton who said: "Power tends to corrupt and absolute power corrupts absolutely." He puts that together with Ronald Reagan's quote: "Politics is supposed to be the second-oldest profession. I have come to realize that it bears a very close resemblance to the first." Bob Beadles does not intend to spend enough time in politics to become a political prostitute. One term will be enough. The author began writing for as a Detroit Examiner (Political Analyst) for Examiner.com for about five years, now serving as an accredited independent freelancer with his own volume releases titled, "Conservative vs. Liberal Ideologies and Applied Economics".

The writer has been televised in Michigan on APNTVMedia.com (Tape 37).

Reference Books

1) *Market For Liberty* by Morris Tannehill and Linda Tannehill
2) *Economics in One Lesson* by Henry Hazlett: "Politics is supposed to be the second-oldest profession. I have come to realize that it bears a very close resemblance to the first."
3) *The Creature from Jekyll Island* by G. Edward Griffin
4) *The Invisible Heart: An Economic Romance* by Russell Roberts
5) *The Vision of the Anointed Self-Congratulation as a Basis for Social Policy* by Thomas Sowell
6) *The True Believer: Thoughts on the Nature of Mass Movements* by Eric Hoffer
7) *Capitalism: The Unknown Ideal* by Ayn Rand, Nathaniel Braden, Alan Greenspan and Robert Hessen
8) *Atlas Shrugged* by Ayn Rand
9) *Deep Cover* by Michael Levine
10) *The Murder of Vince Foster* by Michael Kellett

A Little Political Humor

What is the difference between the Panama Canal and Hillary Clinton? The Panama Canal is a busy ditch.

How can you tell when Bill Clinton is lying? His lips are moving.

Jimmy Carter is considered to have had a failed presidency but he had one major success. He caused a mass exodus of prostitutes from Washington, D.C. They were tired of working for peanuts.

A woman from Detroit died and found herself standing at the pearly gates in front of Saint Peter. She noticed that there were a large number of clocks on the other side of the pearly gates. She asked Saint Peter what the clocks were for and Saint Peter said: "Every person on earth has a clock. It clicks one minute when someone lies. The minute hand on Mother Theresa's clock never moved. Mahatma Ghandi's moved two minutes. The woman said, "What about Kwame Kilpatrick's clock? Saint Peter said, "Jesus uses it as a ceiling fan."

Conservative vs. Liberal Ideologies and Applied Economics

Social Wealth and the Poverty of Tyranny

Volume 1

by Bob Beadles

Conservative vs. Liberal Ideologies and Applied Economics

What is the difference in the vision that conservatives have for the United States as opposed to the vision that liberals have for the United States?

The Conservative vision for the United States hinges on the conservative belief that with more freedom everyone is better off.

Let me digress for a moment. In 1860, Frederick Bastiat first wrote about the broken window fallacy. A youngster passing a bakery throws a rock through the bakery window. A crowd gathers and they say what a shame it is that the window was broken.

Then someone in the crowd says that it's really not so bad. The baker is going to have to pay a glacier to repair the window. The glacier is going to then spend the money on items that he wants and in that sense the economy will be stimulated. That is true as far as it goes. What that analysis misses is that the baker would have bought a new suit with the money he has to spend repairing the window. Because of the broken window, the economy is poorer by one suit. No one misses the suit because it was never produced.

That is the same thing that happens when the government confiscates money through taxes. People see what the government is doing with the money but they don't see what would have been produced in the private sector if that money had not been confiscated by the government.

Liberals want to create a situation where if three people are vying for a job that pays $15 an hour and one of those people is a minority group member, the minority group member will get the job. Republicans want to create a situation where if three people are looking for a job, they can all find jobs that pay $30 an hour.

Economics is all about tradeoffs. It is possible to have a booming economy with unlimited job potential or it is possible to have a big and intrusive government. It is not possible to have both.

In "The Politics of Bad Faith", David Horowitz wrote "The slogan Marx inscribed on the banners of the Communist future, "from each according to his ability to each according to his need" is really an expropriated version of Adam Smith's

Invisible Hand, under which the pursuit of individual interest leads to the fulfillment of the interests of all." What liberals fail to understand is that the Invisible Hand of the marketplace works much better than the heavy hand of the government in solving the problems of individuals as well as the problems of society. While Ronald Reagan's tax cuts caused revenue to the government to double, charitable contributions tripled.

All of you have heard the saying: "Give a man a fish and he will eat for a day. Teach a man to fish and he will eat for a lifetime." Conservatives not only want to teach all citizens to fish, conservatives want to make sure that everyone has a fishing pole and they want to make sure that the river is loaded with fish, so that anyone who is willing to fish cannot help catching all the fish he wants. Liberals, on the other hand, want the government to catch all the fish and they want the American people to have to go to the government and ask for a fish. What liberals want is the definition of socialism.

Conservatives want to create a situation where anyone who is willing and able to work can find a well-paying job. Liberals don't want that because it would create a situation where no one would need their liberal programs and no one would need them.

For the first 140 years of this country's existence, all levels of government (federal, state and local) spent less than 10% of the gross domestic product. Today, all levels of government spend almost 50% of the gross domestic product. If the government was stills spending less than 10% of the GDP,

I suspect that a poor person would be someone who could only afford one 6 bedroom home, two Cadillac's and two flat screen TV's.

In the Old Testament, God wanted his chosen people to have a form of government where God was the only sovereign. The Jews pleaded with God to give them a king and God finally relented and gave them a king.

When the founding fathers of the United States set up the United States government based on the Constitution of the United States, they gave this country the kind of government that God wanted his chosen people to have. Liberals do not like this form of government because with this form of government God is the only Lord and Master of the American people. Liberals want to be the Lords and Masters of the American people. They have gone a long way towards this end by increasing the amount of money that the government spends. To paraphrase Milton Freidman: If the government controls the economy, it controls the life of the individual citizen. The late priest, exorcist and author Malachi Martin said that God continually offers us His Love but that offer is meaningless unless individuals have the freedom to accept or reject that Love. This implies a need for personal and economic freedom. The founding fathers understood that need for freedom. If you hear a liberal talking about the founding fathers of this country, you'll notice that they don't say anything positive about them. There is a reason for this. The Constitution and government that the founding fathers gave this country is the exact opposite of what liberals believe in.

The religion of liberals is big government. Most of the citizens of the United States are Christians. Why do you think that liberals oppose prayer in schools?

Why do liberals oppose public displays of the 10 Commandments? Christianity flies in the face of the religion of big government.

What conservatives offer all the citizens of this country is the freedom to live their lives as they wish to live them.

Sarah Palin and Ron Paul
vs. The Old Guard

A maxim in political science is that a two party system results in a choice between Tweedledee and Tweedledum.

In 2008, the United States two party system resulted in a choice between Dumb and Dumber, with Dumber winning.

George H. W. Bush, Bob Dole, George W. Bush and John McCain have been nominated by Republicans in the last 6 presidential elections. The difference between them and Democrats is minimal.

In 1980 and 1984, when Ronald Reagan ran against Jimmy Carter and then Carter's former Vice President Walter Mondale, the political parties gave the American people the choice between a true conservative and a liberal. Both times, Reagan, the true conservative, won in a landslide.

The old guard of the Republican Party does not favor true conservatives which is why they consistently attack Sarah Palin and Ron Paul.

In 2012, a Palin-Paul ticket would probably win in a landslide just like Ronald Reagan in 1980.

One of the reasons for Ronald Reagan's landslide victory in 1980 was the buffoonery of the Carter administration. Jimmy Carter spawned the Reagan Democrats.

Many conservative pundits, like Rush Limbaugh and Glenn Beck, said that electing Barack Obama would be like giving Jimmy Carter a second term.

Like Carter, Barack Obama has set the stage for a landslide Republican victory if the Republicans nominate a true conservative for president in 2012.

The old guard of the Republican Party has been floating names like Jeb Bush as the next potential Republican nominee. The last this country needs is another Bush as the Republican nominee or as president.

True conservative and tea party members will have to apply consistent pressure on the Republican Party to get a true conservative nominated for president in 2012.

The Assassination of Louis McFadden

On July 21, 2008, Richard C. Cook, a featured writer at Dandelion Salad wrote:

"Dr. Ron Paul, the Republican candidate for the 2008 presidential nomination, is not the first U.S. politician to point to the abuses of the Federal Reserve System and call for its abolishment. Similar pleas to get rid of the Fed were made by Reps. Wright Patman (1893-1976) and Henry Gonzales (1916-2000), both Democratic congressmen from Texas and chairmen of the House Banking Committee.

Few recall, however, how controversial the Fed was when it was first proposed and then maneuvered through a recessing Congress just before Christmas 1913. Rep. Charles Lindbergh, Sr., R-MN and father of the future aviator, called the Federal Reserve Act "the worst legislative crime of the ages."

But the strongest opposition came later, during the Great Depression. The source was Rep. Louis T. McFadden, a Republican representative from Pennsylvania who, as a former bank cashier and president, knew the financial system intimately."

Rep McFadden said:

"When the Federal Reserve Act was passed, the people of these United States did not perceive that a world banking system was being set up here. A super-state controlled by international bankers and industrialists...acting together to enslave the world...Every effort has been made by the Fed to conceal its powers but the truth is--the Fed has usurped the government."

Again from Richard C. Cook:

"McFadden may have paid with his life for his outspokenness. After he lost his congressional seat in 1934, he remained in the public eye as a vigorous opponent of the financial system; that is, until his sudden death on October 3, 1936, of a "dose" of "intestinal flu" after attending a banquet in New York City."

There were two previous attempts on Louis McFadden's life. Two bullets were fired at him on one occasion and later he was poisoned at a banquet.

Again form Richard C. Cook:

"Evidently the third time the assassins succeeded, and the most articulate critic of the Federal Reserve and the financiers' control of the nation was dead. He was 60 years old."

Were international bankers responsible for the assassination of Louis T. McFadden?

Planks of Communism

Norman Mattoon Thomas (November 20, 1884 – December 19, 1968) was a leading American socialist, pacifist, and six-time presidential candidate for the Socialist Party of America.

The Socialist Party candidate for President of the US, Norman Thomas, said this in a 1944 speech:

"The American people will never knowingly adopt socialism. But, under the name of "liberalism," they will adopt every fragment of the socialist program, until one day America will be a socialist nation, without knowing how it happened."

He went on to say: "I no longer need to run as a Presidential Candidate for the Socialist Party. The Democrat Party has adopted our platform."

What Do Tea Party Activists Want?

As the tea party movement gains strength and momentum, its members are being called radical and revolutionary.

What is the truth?

Tea party members like most conservatives and libertarians believe that people are much better off if they have enough money to take care of all their problems by themselves.

Progressives believe that people are better off if the government takes care of their problems for them.

Progressives are oblivious to the teachings of classical and neoclassical economists who contend that an activist government can do no possible good. Progressives are also oblivious to the fact that history has proven classical and neoclassical economists to be correct.

In "Capitalism: the Unknown Ideal" Ayn Rand wrote:

"The trader and the warrior have been fundamental antagonists throughout history. Trade does not flourish on battlefields, factories do not produce under bombardments, profits do not grow on rubble. Capitalism is a society of *traders*—for which it has been denounced by every would-be gunman who regards trade as "selfish" and conquest as "noble.""

Obviously progressives like Barack Obama and Joe Biden do not respect traders since they want to loot all earnings of productive members of society and give those earnings to other people they consider more deserving of that money.

Apologists for big government tout all of the supposed benefits of big government. They neglect all the problems caused by big government. Those problems include recessions, depressions, unemployment, crime and poverty.

In 1959, in an interview with Mike Wallace, Ayn Rand posited that:

"A free economy will not break down. All depressions are caused by government interference and the cure that is always offered . . . is more of the same poisons that caused the disasters."

The Creature

I have read that, in the distant past, there was a time when it was possible for a well-educated person to know everything that was known up to that point in time.

Since that time, there has been an explosion of knowledge.

Today, there is no way one person could keep up with the advances in knowledge in even one subject such as science or literature.

There is one exception to the above statement. One person can easily know everything that needs to be known in economics. That is because there have been no substantive advances in economics for well over 200 years.

Adam Smith died in 1790. He understood that a laissez faire capitalist economy was the most productive type of economic system. In "The Wealth of Nations", he said that the wealth of a nation consists of the goods and services it produces not the gold and silver it possesses.

A person who reads "Basic Economics" by Thomas Sowell, "Applied Economics" by Thomas Sowell, "Economics in One Lesson" by Henry Hazlitt and "The Invisible Heart" by Russell Roberts will know more about economics than most college professors.

What do those books explain? They explain classical economic theory and why it works.

Everything that classical economists have written about was understood by Adam Smith. More recent economists have applied classical economic theory to more modern concepts. Classical economists have always believed in freedom and a free market.

Why are our politicians not applying classical economic theories to the United States economy? "The Creature from Jekyll Island" by G. Edward Griffin explains why.

The creature is the Federal Reserve System.

Keynesians and other left leaning economists do not believe in freedom. They believe in more government and less freedom. Empirical evidence always proves them wrong.

When Keynesians make an economic prediction, they almost always use the caveat "Ceteris Paribus" which literally translate to "All other things being equal". What they mean is if nothing changes they will be correct. The economy is dynamic not static so the snap shot of the economy we see today will be different by tomorrow. That partially explains why Keynesians are so consistently wrong.

What government activities are essential to an economic system? Protection against force and fraud are necessary. Providing a common currency and patent protection are also necessary.

Why are all levels of government involved in areas where they are not needed?

The Creature knows!

Drugs and Bankers

"Deep Cover" by Michael Levine was published in 1990.

Here is a review from The State Journal of Frankfort, Kentucky:

"Fact: The U.S. government traffics narcotics, and also lets drug-dealing nations and cartels go unmolested, if it is the politically expedient thing to do. Yet at the same time, the Federal government was at the time of writing, and still is today, waging a "War on Drugs." As most knowledgeable Americans are now aware, this was a facade, and much more distressing, an act of hypocrisy. The so-called War on Drugs has allowed the U.S. government to further erode citizens' rights, unjustly seize property, and further establish a 1984ish "Big Brother," America. This book should be read.

Bob Beadles

"Deep Cover" details how Michael Levine infiltrated a Mexican drug cartel and discovered that the drug cartel had ties to the highest levels of the Mexican government.

After Michael Levine reported what he had learned to his superiors, Edwin Meese, then U.S. Attorney General called the president of Mexico and blew Michael Levine's cover.

Years later, George W. Bush had two border patrol agents put in jail for doing their duty and shooting a Mexican drug smuggler in the back side.

In "Deep Cover", Michaels Levine said that major banks in the United States would lose a large amount of money if drug trafficking were stopped.

Currently congress is holding a mock investigation of Goldman Sachs because Goldman Sachs has obviously made profits at the expense of most of the other citizens.

This mock investigation is not going to cause any problems for Goldman Sachs.

Progressive politicians in both political parties are bought and paid for by international bankers and their corporate allies with names like Rockefeller, Rothschild, Goldman and Sachs.

These politicians include Obama, McCain, Pelosi, Frank, almost all Democrats and many Republicans.

Progressive politicians claim to be allies of the little guy like rank and file union members but they do the bidding of their owners.

How else would people like the Clintons become multimillionaires when they were not wealthy before entering politics?

The Invention Secrecy Act of 1951

A woman dies and finds herself facing St. Peter at the pearly gates. She says: "Is my husband up here? His name is Frank Smith."

St. Peter says: "There are a lot of Frank Smith's up here."

Mrs. Smith said: "When he was dying, he said that if I ever went out with another man he would roll over in his grave.

St. Peter says: "Oh, you mean old pinwheel Frank."

I suspect that many of the founding fathers have been spinning in their graves since 1951. That is when the Invention Secrecy Act of 1951 was put in place.

The Invention Secrecy Act of 1951 gives the federal government eminent domain over intellectual property.

Eminent domain over real property is bad enough but eminent domain over intellectual property is ridiculous.

From Wikipedia, the free encyclopedia:

The Invention Secrecy Act of 1951, codified at 35 U.S.C. § 181–188 (Title 35, Chapter 17 of the United States Code), is a body of United States federal law designed to prevent disclosure of new inventions and technologies that, in the opinion of selected federal agencies, present a possible threat to the national security of the United States.

The U.S. government has long sought to control the release of new technologies that might threaten the national defense and economic stability of the country. During World War I, Congress authorized the United States Patent and Trademark Office (PTO) to classify certain defense-related patents. This initial effort lasted only for the duration of that war but was reimposed in October 1941 in anticipation of the U.S. entry into World War II. Patent secrecy orders were initially intended to remain effective for two years, beginning on July 1, 1940, but were later extended for the duration of the war.

The Invention Secrecy Act of 1951 made such patent secrecy permanent. Under this Act, defense agencies provide the PTO with a classified list of sensitive technologies in the form of the "Patent Security Category Review List" (PSCRL). The decision to classify new inventions under this act is made by "defense agencies" as defined by the President. Generally, these agencies include the Army, Navy, Air Force, National

Security Agency (NSA), Department of Energy, and NASA, but even the Justice Department has played this role.

A secrecy order bars the award of a patent, orders that the invention be kept secret, restricts the filing of foreign patents, and specifies procedures to prevent disclosure of ideas contained in the application. The only way an inventor can avoid the risk of such imposed secrecy is to forgo patent protection.

By the end of fiscal year 1991, the number of patent secrecy orders stood at 6,193. Many such orders were imposed on individuals and organizations working without government support. This number shrank for each fiscal year thereafter, until 2002. Since 2002, the number of secrecy orders has grown, with 5,002 secrecy orders in effect at the end of fiscal year 2007.

The types of inventions classified under this Act is itself a secret, but most of the inventions which are now no longer secret but once were secret have been in areas with high military significance, such as cryptography and weapons development.

The Invention Secrecy Act of 1951 allows the government to steal any invention they choose to steal.

In "Liberal Fascism", Jonah Goldberg says that big government and big business have been working together to enrich themselves and take everything they can steal from everyone else since 1913. What a great tool the Invention

Secrecy Act of 1951 is for that theft.

ASA Publishing Corporation

Ayn Rand and Alan Greenspan

Ayn Rand was a champion of individual freedom. Her best known books dramatized the fight between statists and individualists. The most popular books were works of fiction including "Anthem", "Atlas Shrugged" and" The Fountainhead". "The Fountainhead" was made into a great movie starring Gary Cooper.

Statists believe that government should control the life of the individual. They believe that all rights are and should be derived from the government.

Individualists believe in individual freedom in every area of life. They believe as Thomas Jefferson said "When the people fear the government, there is tyranny. When the government fears the people, there is liberty."

One of Ayn Rand's lesser known books is a collection of essays on capitalism and freedom. It is titled, "Capitalism: the Unknown Ideal" published in 1966. Three of the chapters in this book were written by an Ayn Rand disciple named Alan Greenspan. One of those chapters was about the importance of a country having a gold standard.

For years, Alan Greenspan campaigned to eliminate the Federal Reserve System and bring back the gold standard.

In 1987, Alan Greenspan was appointed Chairman of the Fed. He stayed in that post until 2006.

What happened? I believe that Alan Greenspan sold out. I suspect that Alan Greenspan could give Benedict Arnold lessons in how to betray one's own country.

Others have a kinder view of Alan Greenspan. I recall a guest on the late Mark Scott's radio show saying, "Alan Greenspan believes in Alan Greenspan uber alles."

What he was saying was the Alan Greenspan's ego was so large that he believed that he could do as good a job or maybe even a better job of protecting the country's currency than a gold standard.

Why did Alan Greenspan go over to the dark side? Only Alan Greenspan can answer that question.

State's Rights

The 10th amendment to the constitution of the United reads: "The powers not delegated to the United States by the Constitution, nor prohibited by it to the States, are reserved to the States respectively, or to the people."

Recently politicians within state governments have been citing the 10th Amendment and saying the federal government is infringing on state's rights with their laws and unfunded mandates.

The following two paragraphs were written by David M. Dickson in the Washington Times in 2009:

"Worried the federal government is increasing its dominance over their affairs, several states are pursuing legislative action to assert their sovereignty under the 10th Amendment of the Constitution in hopes of warding off demands from Washington on how to spend money or enact policy. The growing concerns even have a handful of governors questioning whether to accept federal stimulus money that comes with strings attached.

The sentiments to declare themselves legally independent from Washington have swept across as many as a dozen states, renewing a debate over so-called unfunded mandates that last raged in the 1990s. The states question whether the U.S. government can force states to take actions without paying for them or impose conditions on states if they accept certain federal funding."

The 10th Amendment is not the tool state legislators are attempting to use in order to free themselves from the yoke of the federal government.

In Montana, in 2008 state legislators said that if the Supreme Court ruled that the 2nd Amendment did not apply to individuals that it violated Montana's agreement to join the union and that Montana would at that point secede from the union.

Recently South Carolina state representative introduced legislation that would mandate gold and silver coins replace Federal Reserve Notes in South Carolina.

It looks like a nonviolent revolution may have started.

Government Spending and Ron Paul

Spending, at all levels of government, is totally out of control.

What is needed is a complete overhaul at all levels of government.

To ensure a sound currency, the Federal Reserve System needs to be eliminated and a gold standard restored.

There is evidence that the 16th Amendment was never legally ratified. A president with the courage to do it could site that evidence and eliminate the 16th Amendment with an executive order. The 16th Amendment authorizes the income tax, the Internal Revenue Service and the Bureau of Alcohol, Tobacco and Firearms.

The next step would be to eliminate all taxes within the United States and replace them with a 6% sales tax to be split three ways between federal, state and local units of government.

According to usgovernmentspending.com, in 2008 the

federal government spent 37.12% of the gross domestic product.

How could government spending be cut so drastically?

Most government spending and agencies do nothing to improve the lives of United States citizens. The federal government has over one thousand regulatory agencies. If those agencies were eliminated the only people adversely affected would be the people working for those agencies.

The Department of Education has done nothing to improve education. The Department of Energy has done nothing to increase energy production.

The federal government could easily be pared down to $1/10^{th}$ its current size and still perform all its essential functions.

The federal government also gives money to organizations that do nothing to benefit the United States. These organizations include the United Nations, the International Monetary Fund and the World Bank.

Significantly downsizing the U.S. government would cause the kind of boom that would result in anyone who is willing and able to work having a well-paying job. After the initial downsizing government revenue would increase year after year.

What about Social Security? The federal government owns over 30% of the land in the United States. They could sell that land and give the people receiving social security annuities that would pay more than their social security checks.

Do we currently have any potential presidential candidates who would have the courage to do what needs to be done to save this country? Ron Paul would.

The Party of the Super Rich

Democrats claim that Republicans are the party of the rich when Democrats are the party of the super rich.

Billionaire George Soros is a Democrat. Politician Jay Rockefeller is the great grandson of oil tycoon John D. Rockefeller.

Recently Democrat Jay Rockefeller said:

"I'm tired of the right and the left, "There's a little bug inside of me which wants to get the FCC to say to Fox and to MSNBC, 'Out. Off. End. Goodbye."

The following statements were made on December 7th:

Billionaire investor and philanthropist George Soros

warned tonight in New York that the combination of Fox News, Glenn Beck, The Tea Party, and the ability of Americans to fantasize unrealistically about their political system might lead "this open society to be on the verge of some dictatorial democracy."

Soros mentioned George Orwell's novel, "1984" as a possible precedent for the kind of fantasies being promulgated in our culture today. Orwell's "1984" satirized the Communist system of absolute control over society and politics that prevailed in the Soviet Union until 1990.

What do the comments of Rockefeller and Soros have in common? They show a distain for the free press.

Rush Limbaugh, Glenn Beck and members of the tea party movement are openly talking about the problems caused by Democrats at the behest of the super rich.

The super rich of the world do not like the fact that the United States has always had a middle class that pays no attention to what the super rich believe or want.

The super rich of the world want to destroy the middle class.

That would leave only the super rich and the poor. The

lives of the poor would then be totally controlled by the super rich. That is what the push for a one world government is all about.

Every Democrat is in favor of a one world government. That is also true of liberal Republicans.

After visiting China, David Rockefeller Sr., Jay Rockefeller's uncle, praised Mao Tse-tung, who slaughtered over 40 million of his own people, with the following quote:

"One is impressed immediately by the sense of national harmony . . . Whatever the price of the Chinese Revolution it has obviously succeeded . . . in fostering high morale and community purpose. General social and economic progress is no less impressive . . . The enormous social advances of China have benefited greatly from the singleness of ideology and purpose . . . **The social experiment in China under Chairman Mao's leadership is one of the most important and successful in history.**" -*New York Times*, 8-10-1973."

The super rich like the Rockefellers and George Soros want to set up the type of class system that was in place for most of the world's history. People were born into wealth or poverty. They were born into an upper or lower class. People had no opportunity to raise themselves out of their social class or their economic state.

The super rich want to create a situation where

everyone else has to kneel and bow when they pass by.

Tea party candidates, many of whom are supported by Fox News, Rush Limbaugh and Glenn Beck, are preparing to wrest control of Congress away from politicians who are owned by the super rich. This development is very upsetting to people like Jay Rockefeller and George Soros.

Laws of Nature and Politicians

True conservatives believe that there are immutable universal laws of nature and science that are always in effect. True conservatives realize that they must operate within the boundaries of these laws.

Newton's third law of motion states "For every action there is an equal and opposite reaction". Conservative economists apply that law to economics by saying "There is no free lunch." That means every action the government takes affects something in the private sector. Since all wealth is created in the private sector, when the government sucks wealth out of the private sector, the private sector produces less wealth. That means fewer jobs, lower wages and higher prices. Economics is all about trade- offs. A country may have a booming economy that produces the maximum amount of wealth possible or it may have a large and intrusive government with a less robust economy. The larger the government the more depressed the economy will be.

What does the government do? The government transfers wealth and it makes rules and regulations that apply to the private sector. These activities produce no wealth but they consume large amounts of wealth because the bureaucrats working for the government have to be well paid or they will find better paying jobs in the private sector.

As George Washington said "Government is not reason, it is not eloquence; it is force. Like fire it is a dangerous servant and a fearful master". Washington was not saying that government is not necessary. He was saying that government has very limited functions and that government needs to be tightly controlled. The September 28 edition of the Detroit Free Press provided s great example of out of control government. The Department of Environmental Quality prosecuted a business owner in Sparta Michigan for paving over a mud puddle. Hart Enterprises employs 100 people and the DEQ may be chasing Hart Enterprises out of Michigan. Why is that happening? It is because people, who are not politicians, bureaucrats or judges, do not have enough control over the DEQ. As Lord Acton said "Power corrupts and absolute power corrupts absolutely." True conservatives believe that bureaucrats should be public servants not lords and masters of the public. They know that government excess needs to be curbed. As Ronald Reagan said: "Government is like a baby; an alimentary canal with a big appetite at one end and no sense of responsibility at the other."

Republicans were losers the 2008 presidential race because the powers that be in the Republican Party were unwilling to run a true conservative for the office of president. Few people at the grass roots level wanted John McCain as the president.

John McCain is the choice and responsibility of the Rockefeller Republicans. Who are the Rockefeller Republicans? They are the establishment Republicans who want politicians and bureaucrats to be lords and masters of the people. Big government serves the people who already have wealth and helps to prevent the people who are not wealthy from catching up with the already wealthy.

Why do liberals resort to ad homonym attacks and name calling instead of using logical arguments to confound their foes? Liberals suffer from logic envy. Their beliefs cannot be proven logically so they must resort to other tactics in order to win. Liberals are notorious for their staunch belief in ideas and theories that are confounding to most conservatives. For example, people in liberal environmental groups believe that clear cutting of forests is wrong. Clear cutting removes the dead and most combustible wood from the forests. That makes it much easier to contain forest fires. Environmental groups say that clear cutting is not natural because forests do not clear cut themselves. That is like saying that living in a house is not natural because houses do not build themselves.

Like liberals, Rockefeller Republicans cannot publicly explain what they believe in. To do that honestly they would have to say "We want it all and we don't care what happens to anyone else." Rockefeller Republicans may be smarter than liberals but they do no more to benefit the general public than liberals.

It should be easy for anyone to spot a true conservative. True conservatives use logical arguments to prove what they believe in and they buttress their arguments with historically documented proof. For example, every time tax rates have been cut, the United States economy has expanded.

End the Fed

Ron Paul has written a book titled "End the Fed".

What is the Fed? It is the Federal Reserve System.

What is the Federal Reserve System? It is the central bank of the United States.

What is a central bank? It is a private for profit bank that controls a country's money supply.

What did Thomas Jefferson think of the idea of the United States having a central bank?

"The [privately-owned] Central Bank is an institution of the most deadly hostility existing against the principles and form of our Constitution . . . if the American people allow private banks to control the issuance of their currency, first by inflation and then by deflation, the banks and corporations that will grow up around them will deprive the people of all their property until their children will wake up homeless on the continent their fathers conquered."

The Federal Reserve System was not the first central bank in the history of the United States. In fact, it was called the Federal Reserve System because there were too many people still living who remembered the previous central bank of the United States when it was put in place.

The Federal Reserve System was put in place in1913, the year Woodrow Wilson was inaugurated. What did Woodrow Wilson think of this accomplishment?

"I am a most unhappy man. I have unwittingly ruined my country. A great industrial nation is controlled by its system of credit. Our system of credit is concentrated. The growth of the nation, therefore, and all our activities are in the hands of a few men. We have come to be one of the worst ruled, one of the most completely controlled and dominated Governments in the civilized world no longer a Government by free opinion, no longer a Government by conviction and the vote of the majority, but a Government by the opinion and duress of a small group of dominant men." -Woodrow Wilson, after signing the Federal Reserve into existence

Finally, more and more citizens are becoming aware of the problems caused by the Federal Reserve System.

If the dollar crashes, it will be due to the Federal Reserve System. Why would the Fed want to crash the dollar and ruin the U. S. economy? Forcing the United States to accept a one world currency and forcing the U.S. into a one world government would only increase the power of international bankers.

Big Government is Bad Government

If the founding fathers of the United States were alive today, almost all of them would be Libertarians.

Libertarians believe that big government is bad government. Why?

1) Bureaucrats consistently prove Lord Acton's maxim: "Power corrupts. Absolute power corrupts absolutely." People who have had to deal with bureaucrats know bureaucrats like to throw their weight around.

2) Big government gives politicians something to sell and always leads to political corruption. What politicians sell is protection. A great example of the government selling protection is "Prohibition". John D. Rockefeller, the founder of the Standard Oil Company, said "Competition is a sin." John D. Rockefeller was one of the biggest proponents of "Prohibition". Why?

Henry Ford made his first automobile so they ran on either alcohol or gasoline. "Prohibition" made it illegal to produce alcohol for any reason.

3) Big government wastes large amounts of money and produces nothing that adds to a nation's gross domestic product. Even agencies that should benefit the public offer little or no benefit. For example, the Department of Education has done nothing to improve education and the Department of Energy has not kept down the price of energy or produced any energy.

   If the money wasted by government were left in the private sector, the gross domestic product would grow exponentially and everyone in this country would be richer as a result.

4) Imagine a situation where a person could go out and earn as much money as that person wanted to earn. The restrictions of big government make that kind of situation impossible.

   The problems created by big government are almost endless. In fact, virtually every problem faced by the United States is due to big government and the Federal Reserve System. The federal government put the fed in place.

McCarthyism

The name Joe McCarthy is synonymous with the term McCarthyism. Why and what does McCarthyism mean?

Wikipedia offers this definition of McCarthyism: **"McCarthyism** is the politically motivated practice of making accusations of disloyalty, subversion, or treason without proper regard for evidence. The term specifically describes activities associated with the period in the United States known as the Second Red Scare, lasting roughly from the late 1940s to the late 1950s and characterized by heightened fears of communist influence on American institutions and espionage by Soviet agents. Originally coined to criticize the anti-communist pursuits of U.S. Senator Joseph McCarthy, "McCarthyism" soon took on a broader meaning, describing the excesses of similar efforts. The term 's also now used more generally to describe reckless, unsubstantiated accusations, as well as <u>demagogic</u> attacks on the character or patriotism of political adversaries."

What was Senator McCarthy really trying to do? He wanted to make sure that no member of the communist party had access to sensitive material that would be valuable to the Soviet Union.

Why does Joe McCarthy have such a terrible reputation? He has been relentlessly smeared by the left in this country ever since he brought down Alger Hiss. Alger Hiss was a favorite of the American left. Alger Hiss was an employee of the State Department when his former friend Whittaker Chambers accused him of being a communist.

Franklin Delano Roosevelt and Harry Truman often spoke of Uncle Joe. They weren't referring to Joe McCarthy. They were referring to Joe Stalin. Roosevelt and Truman despised Joe McCarthy.

Most Americans do not realize that when Joe McCarthy died 30,000 American lined up in front of the church where he was lying in state to pay tribute to him. They do not realize that his wife received 70 mailbags full of condolence letters and cards.

The same smear tactics that the left used against Joe McCarthy were also used against Richard Nixon.

What did Richard Nixon do to the left?

Ben Shalom Bernanke

Ben Shalom Bernanke was born on December 13, 1953. He succeeded Alan Greenspan as Chairman of the Federal Reserve on February 1, 2006.

The following quote is from Wikipedia: "Bernanke is particularly interested in the economic and political causes of the <u>Great Depression</u>, on which he has written extensively. Before Bernanke's work, the dominant <u>monetarist</u> theory of the Great Depression was <u>Milton Friedman's</u> view that it had been largely caused by the <u>Federal Reserve's</u> having reduced the <u>money supply</u>. In a speech on Milton Friedman's ninetieth birthday (November 8, 2002), Bernanke said, "Let me end my talk by abusing slightly my status as an official representative of the Federal Reserve. I would like to say to Milton and Anna [Schwartz, Friedman's coauthor]: Regarding the Great Depression. You're right, we did it. We're very sorry. But thanks to you, we won't do it again." Anna Schwartz however is highly critical of Bernanke and wrote an opinion piece on New York Times to advise President Obama against his reappointment to Chair of Federal Reserve."

What Mr. Bernanke did not confess, regarding the Great Depression, was that the Fed created a large economic bubble by expanding the money supply much faster than the economy was growing. That caused a great deal of artificial growth. When the Fed decreased the money supply the bubble burst and the stock market crashed. The stock market crash, followed by the disastrous policies of Herbert Hoover led to the Great Depression. Then, the inept policies of Franklin Delano Roosevelt prolonged the Great Depression for 8 more years. (For more information on the policies of FDR, see "FDR's Folly" by Jim Powell and "New Deal or Raw Deal" by Burton W. Folsom Jr.

As long as the money supply grows no faster than the economy, there are no economic bubbles and no inflation.

The boom and bust cycles that some people call the business cycle are caused directly by the Fed's expansion and sometime contraction of the money supply.

Roads and Bridges

On April 19, staff writers at the Monroe Evening News wrote:

"Some of the high-traffic, paved roads in southeast Michigan are getting better, but the roads rated in poor condition are getting worse.

That's the summary the annual statewide asset management rating system released this month by the Southeast Michigan Council of Governments (SEMCOG). "

"This survey data confirm what users of our transportation infrastructure already know," said Carmine Palombo, director of transportation programs at SEMCOG. "The condition of our roads continues to deteriorate."

The study shows about 18.5% percent of the 4,300 miles of the paved, federal-aid-eligible roads in southeast Michigan were in good condition last year, compared to just 13% percent the year before. That means some of the region's roads, like I-75, I-275 or Telegraph Rd., were paved or were improved. But, 34% percent of those roads are now in poor condition, compared to just 30% percent in poor condition the year before.

"That's not going to change," said Howard Penrod, director of the Monroe County Road Commission. "That's not going to change unless there is some kind of change in the funding formula. Our roads are going to continue to get worse unless something is done about it. '"

Most citizens on both the left and right consider keeping roads and bridges in good repair a legitimate function of government. That is because keeping roads and bridges in good repair affects the safety of the citizens.

Unfortunately, government at all levels spends a great deal of money on activities that are better left to the private sector.

If all nonessential and illegitimate activities of government were eliminated, government would spend more time and money on keeping roads and bridges in good repair.

Nonessential activities of government include regulatory enforcement, charity, employment services, housing services and the list goes on and on.

Richard Nixon

Like Joe McCarthy, Richard Nixon has been relentlessly smeared by the left both prior to and after the Watergate hearings. The left started smearing Nixon at the same time they started smearing Joe McCarthy. The reason the smear campaign started is that while Joe McCarthy was a Senator Richard Nixon was a member of the House of Representatives. Richard Nixon was as instrumental in proving that Alger Hiss was a communist as Joe McCarthy.

With the Watergate hearings, the left finally succeeded in hounding Richard Nixon out of office. The left has succeeded in creating the impression that Watergate was all about Richard Nixon. It was not.

In "Silent Coup", Len Colodny and Robert Gettlin offer proof that the Watergate break in was totally a John Dean operation. Why was john Dean interested in breaking into the

Democrat National Committee headquarters in the Watergate hotel? Prior to the Watergate break in, a call girl ring with ties to the Democrat National Committee was busted. Maureen Biner was one of those call girls and the secretary of the DNC keep Maureen Biner's picture, name and phone number in her desk. John Dean married Maureen Biner one week before the Watergate hearings began.

There are many layers to the Watergate onion that have never been peeled.

E. Howard Hunt, a former CIA agent and member of the Nixon administration, was one of the original suspects in the killing of John F. Kennedy and then he ends up in the middle of Watergate

James W. McCord, a former CIA agent, was the Watergate burglar who taped over a normally locked door and when a watchman ripped off the tape, McCord taped the door again. How would a trained CIA agent do something that stupid if he did not want to get caught?

After the Watergate break in and before John Dean placed the blame for Watergate on Richard Nixon was there any contact between Hunt, McCord and Dean?

Knowledge

On December 2, 2009, Walter E. Williams wrote an article titled "The Pretense of Knowledge".

"The ultimate constraint that we all face is knowledge - what we know and don't know. The knowledge problem is pervasive and by no means trivial as hinted at by just a few examples. You've purchased a house. Was it the best deal you could have gotten? Was there some other house you could have purchased that 10 years later would not have needed extensive repairs or was in a community with more likeable neighbors and a better environment for your children? What about the person you married? Was there another person who would have made for a more pleasing spouse? Though these are important questions, the most intelligent answer you can give to all of them is: "I don't know."

Since you don't know the answers, who do you think, here on Earth, is likely to know and whom would you like to make these decisions for you — Nancy Pelosi, Harry Reid, George Bush, a czar appointed by Obama or a committee of Washington bureaucrats? I bet that if these people were to forcibly make housing or marital decisions for us, most would deem it tyranny."

What Dr. Williams is pointing out is that no one is knowledgeable enough to make those kinds of decisions for other people.

Although no one is knowledgeable enough to make important or life changing decisions for other people that is exactly what the Democrat party is trying to do with Obamacare.

For years, liberal economists have said that the people United States have to get used to a lower standard of living so that the rest of the world can have more. Jimmy carter and his advisers were dumb enough to have Jimmy Carter utter that statement as he campaigned for reelection.

Cap and Trade would give citizens of the United States a much lower standard of living. Despite that fact that the majority of U.S. citizens do not want Cap and Trade, The Democrat Party is poised to give it to us.

Why do Democrats think they are entitled to make such monumental decisions for everyone else? They believe that being liberal makes them intellectually superior to everyone else.

Conspiracy Theories

The common link between most conspiracy theories is that there are persons or organizations attempting to put a one world government in place.

The organizations most often mentioned in conspiracy theories are The Council on Foreign Relations, the Bilderberger Group, and the Trilateral Commission, the Masons and the Skull and Bones fraternity at Yale. According to conspiracy theorists these organizations want to eliminate Christianity, along with the middle class and put a one world government in place.

Why would anyone want to do that? According to the conspiracy theorists, the wealthiest people in the world are not satisfied controlling most of the world's wealth. They want it all.

Are there any other common threads running through

conspiracy theories? Yes, one of the most common threads is that the people and organizations pushing for a one world government have a satanic connection.

The Masons are all about putting a one world government in place.

The late Malachi Martin was a catholic priest, a good friend of Pope John Paul II, an exorcist and the author of 15 books. In "Windswept House", he strongly suggests that, at the top, the Masons are a Satanic organization. In an interview with the late Mark Scott, Malachi Martin said that he did not believe that God would allow a one world government to be put in place because it would be too "Luciferian".

Glenn Beck says that it is obvious that the Obama administration and the Federal Reserve are in the process of crashing the dollar as well as the U.S. economy, so that they can force the U.S. in a one world government.

Saul Alinsky, one of Barack Obama's mentors, wrote a book titled "Rules for Radicals". "Rules for Radicals" was dedicated to Lucifer.

ASA Publishing Corporation

Milton Friedman

Milton Friedman (July 31, 1912 - November 16, 2006) was one of the best known conservative economists of his time. Conservative economists quoted him and liberal economists railed against him. Liberal economists called him the wild man from Chicago and one liberal economist said "The only way to beat Milton Friedman in a debate is to deny him the premise he intends to argue from. If he is given the premise he intends to argue from, he will build an argument that is so sound and logical there is no way to beat him."

Milton Friedman's best known book is "Capitalism and Freedom". The title of the first chapter is: "The relationship between economic freedom and capitalism".

"It is Widely Believed that politics and economics are separate and largely unconnected; that individual freedom is a political problem; and material welfare is an economic problem and that any kind of political arrangements can be combined with any kind of economic arrangements. The chief contemporary manifestation of this idea is the advocacy of "democratic socialism" by many who condemn out of hand the restrictions of individual freedom imposed by "totalitarian socialism" in Russia, and who are persuaded that it is possible for a country to adopt the essential features of Russian economic arrangements and yet to ensure individual freedom through political arrangements. The thesis of this chapter is that such a view is delusion, that there is an intimate connection between economics and politics, that only certain combinations of political and economic arrangements are possible, and that in particular, a society that is socialist cannot be democratic, in the sense of guaranteeing individual freedom."

Why would anyone argue that it is wrong for a person to pursue whatever career or occupation that person desires so long as that pursuit is not injurious to anyone else?

Milton Friedman had the answer to that question.

"Underlying most arguments against the free market is a lack of belief in freedom itself."

The Fed and the United Nations

On November 8, 2002 Ben Bernanke publicly admitted to Milton Friedman that the Federal Reserve System had created the Great depression. Mr. Bernanke finished by saying, "You're right, we did it. We're very sorry. But thanks to you, we won't do it again."

It appears that Mr. Bernanke was lying.

The Federal Reserve System caused the Great Depression by expanding the money supply much faster than the economy was expanding and creating easy credit. Then they shrunk the money supply and made it much more difficult to obtain credit. This action caused loans to be called in and businesses to fail. The stock market crashed and the actions of the government exacerbated the problem leading to the Great Depression.

In recent years, the Federal Reserve System has been expanding the money supply much faster than the economy has been expanding, creating easy credit and also propping up the stock market.

Coupled with the reckless spending of the Obama administration, the actions of the Fed have expanded the money supply well beyond the point where inflation and a credit crunch could become inevitable.

The stage has been set for another stock market crash and possibly another Great Depression.

Why would anyone want to crash the United States economy?

United Nations officials have been complaining the national sovereignty of nations like the United States stands in the way of a one world government.

A depression would put pressure on citizens of the United States to join a one world government.

A one world government would give the international bankers, who control the Federal Reserve System, and the corporate elite of the world total control over the world's wealth and total control over the individual citizens of the world. It would be a dream come true for the greediest people in the world.

Global Warming

People who know my views on man-made global warming consider me to be a man-made global warming denier. I am beginning to worry that this may cause these people to think that I also deny the existence of the Easter bunny, Santa Claus and the tooth fairy.

I believe that most of the problems within the United States are caused by bloated and out of control government at all levels. This has led some people to conclude that I am campaigning for Al Gore since he is also bloated and out of control.

I am wondering what Al Gore will say when someone asks him why Mars is warming at the same rate as the Earth. That evidence comes from NASA's Mars probe. If he is consistent, he will say it is due to the activity of the men on Mars. I doubt that he will mention that the temperature of the sun fluctuates. As the sun gets warmer, the Earth gets warmer. As the sun cools, the Earth cools.

It is not surprising that children believe all the man-made global warming stories but to see adults listen to Al Gore's histrionics while keeping a straight face is truly amazing.

Seeing Al Gore reminds me of a famous quote from Mark Twain: "Suppose you were an idiot and suppose you were a member of Congress. But I repeat myself."

There is evidence that the Earth was much warmer during the Middle Ages than it has been for the last 100 years, according to a Harvard study. If global warming is going to cause catastrophes now, why were there no catastrophes, due to global warming, during the Middle Ages?

A new word needs to be added to the English language. That word is goron. A goron is a person who, despite all the evidence to the contrary, continues to believe in man-made global warming.

Economics is known as the dismal science because of an early economist named Thomas Malthus (1766 – 1834). Malthus predicted that human population would grow exponentially and that the food supply would grow geometrically leading to a food shortage and mass starvation. His solution for this problem was euthanasia for anyone who was too old or disabled to work. He exempted intellectuals like himself.

In 1980, Paul R. Ehrlich recycled the Malthusian Theorem in his book "The Population Bomb". Ehrlich predicted mass starvation due to overpopulation.

People who believe liberal propaganda believe that big government is the solution to the world's problems. Once people catch on to the man-made global warming hoax, we might see the overpopulation scare being recycled again. People who believe the propaganda spewed by liberals like Malthus and Ehrlich pay no heed to the often repeated quote attributed to Thomas Jefferson "A government big enough to give you anything you want is big enough to take everything you've got."

Michigan's Tax Burden

On May 9, 2010 the Monroe published an article by Associated Press writer Kathy Barks Hoffman titled "Times are tough but you're paying less in taxes now".

What Ms. Hoffman fails to explain is that the reason for lower taxes is that the Michigan tax system has destroyed so much of the wealth of Michigan residents.

On February 3, 2010 Michael D. LaFaive wrote on the Mackinac Center for Public Policy website:

"As Gov. Jennifer Granholm approaches her final State of the State address this evening, it is worth taking an unvarnished look at the economic well-being of Michigan. Since she took office, Michigan has experienced:

- A precipitous decline in the relative wealth of its residents. Since January 2003, Michigan's per-capita personal income rank among the states has dropped from 23rd to 37th. Our personal income is now $5,259 (13.1% percent) below the national average.

- A large decline in economic output as measured by state Gross Domestic Product, dropping from 26th at the start of the Granholm administration to 41st through 2008.

- A dramatic increase in unemployment. Michigan's unemployment rate leapt from 6.7% percent in January 2003 to 14.6% percent through December 2009. The state has had the highest unemployment rate in the nation for 46 consecutive months.

- Record setting out-migration. The U.S. Census Bureau reports that Michigan has lost population for the last four years in a row and was only one of two states to lose population last year. More than 87,000 people migrated from the state between July 2008 and July 2009 alone. United Van Lines — a household moving company — reports that 68% percent of all its Michigan-related traffic is outbound.

Remarkably, Michigan suffered economic decline even during the last national expansion, from 2002 through 2007."

The state of Michigan has done nothing to lessen the tax burden on its citizens.

Citizens of Michigan have simply become poorer because so many employers have left Michigan or downsized their businesses.

Many employers have left Michigan so that they would not have to deal with unions. Most right to work states not only protect businesses from union harassment, they also have lower tax rates than the state of Michigan.

Foreign Precedent in the Legal System

"Something is always lost in the translation." This old saying is almost always true.

The most famous words written by Rene Descartes are:

"Cogito ergo sum.' From Latin to English that translates to "I think therefore I am.' It was the convention of Descartes time to write all scholarly work in Latin. Descartes was French and what Descartes wrote in French translates to English as, "As I think, so I am."

The English bible was translated from other languages including Hebrew, Aramaic, Greek and Latin.

Most people have learned in church or in school that the sixth commandment says, "Thou shalt not kill." A better translation from the original Aramaic is. "Do no murder." That means killing is allowed in certain circumstances such as self-defense, defending one's family or defending one's country.

Some people on the political left, including some members of the Supreme Court, are saying that American courts should consider precedents set in foreign courts when considering cases in United States courts.

In France, the Napoleonic code is the law of the land. Former French president, Charles de Gaulle prevented the popular television courtroom drama-mystery Perry Mason from being shown on French television for fear that it would cause the French people to clamor for a United States type of system of justice.

What possible relevance could decisions in French courts have to decisions being made in courts in the United States?
Using precedents set in foreign courts to influence decisions in United States courts would simply make it easier to circumvent the constitution. There would almost certainly be some purposeful mistranslation.

Ronald Reagan and Jack Hoogendyk

Ronald Reagan was a true conservative.

What is a true conservative? A true conservative believes in small government, defending the homeland against all enemies and no government intrusion in the life of the individual. A true conservative believes that individuals are endowed by their Creator with inalienable rights that no person or government has the right to infringe upon. One of those rights is the right to practice or not practice any given religion. A true conservative stands up for these principles.

Unfortunately, most of the people who call themselves conservatives today are cosmetic conservatives.

What is a cosmetic conservative? A cosmetic conservative is like a harlot who dresses demurely and claims to be a virgin. The harlot's actions speak much louder than her words. Like the harlot, the cosmetic conservative claims to be a true conservative but sells out to whomever or whatever gives instant gratification. Instant gratification can come in many forms. It may come in the form of the liberal media saying that this cosmetic conservative is growing as a person. Read growing as gutless and unprincipled.

Gratification may come in the form of adulation from the cosmetic conservatives' liberal colleagues saying that the cosmetic conservative did the right thing. Read the right thing as forcing the American people bend over and grab their ankles. Gratification may come from receiving more tax dollars for a local project that buys the cosmetic conservative more votes. In the last instance, the cosmetic conservative ignores the fact that constituents are being setting up to have their pockets picked by the government for other projects, in other areas, at a later date.

Ronald Reagan proved that he was a true conservative by cutting taxes, increasing defense spending at a time when defense spending was entirely inadequate and attempting to cut unnecessary domestic spending.

Ronald Reagan was the last true conservative to run for president.

John McCain was so far to the left he did not even qualify as a cosmetic conservative.

Where will the next true conservative to run for public office come from?

We have a true conservative, in the mold of Ronald Reagan, right here in Michigan. His name is Jack Hoogendyk. Jack Hoogendyk would be a great replacement for Jennifer Granholm, Carl Levin or Barack Obama.

2012 and the Mayan Calendar

The earth is a giant magnet.

How does a magnet work? Magnetic flux travels out of the north end of a magnet, turns south and travels back around the magnet and enters the south end of the magnet. That is why the north end of one magnet is attracted to the south end of another magnet. That is also why north ends of two magnets repel each other and the south ends of two magnets repel each other.

As 2012 approaches, an increasing number of people are speculating about why the Mayan calendar ends in 2012. That speculation sometimes includes planet X.

What is planet X? Some scientists believe it to be a dark star with a long elliptical orbit around the sun. They suggest that planet X enters the solar system approximately every 2600 years.

What do the earth's magnetic properties, the Mayan calendar and planet X have to do with each other?

Native American and Mayan lore connect Planet X with many disasters.

There is evidence that the earth's magnetic poles have reversed themselves more than once. What would it take for the earth's magnetic poles to reverse? The earth's magnetic force would have to become very weak and it has been becoming weaker every year. A strong gravitational pull would have to exert itself on the earth. Such a force could conceivably cause the earth to shift on its axis which in and of itself would cause many problems such as earthquakes, volcanic eruptions, tidal waves and floods.

As the earth's poles were reversing, for a time there would be no magnetic flux traveling around the earth. It is magnetic flux that protects the creatures on earth from the rays of the sun. With no magnetic flux protecting the earth, solar flares could prove deadly.

How long will it take politicians to start telling the American people that with higher taxes and more government spending, they can protect us from all the potential dangers coming our way?

Adam Smith vs. John Maynard Keynes

Prior to Adam Smith, all economists were mercantilists. Mercantilists believed that the wealth of a nation consisted of the gold and silver possessed by that nation.

The following paragraph is from Wikipedia:

"An Inquiry into the Nature and Causes of the Wealth of Nations (generally referred to by the short title *The Wealth of Nations*) is the masterpiece of the <u>Scottish</u> economist and moral philosopher <u>Adam Smith</u>. First published in <u>1776</u>, it is a reflection on <u>economics</u> at the beginning of the <u>Industrial Revolution</u> and argues that free market economies are more productive and beneficial to their societies. The book, written for the educated, is considered to be the foundation of modern economic theory."

In "The Wealth of Nations" Adam Smith said that the wealth of a nation consisted of the goods and services produced by that nation rather than the amount of gold and silver possessed by that nation.

Adam Smith said that the invisible hand of the marketplace was sufficient to regulate the marketplace. The forces behind the invisible hand were self-interest and competition along with supply and demand.

The Founding fathers of the United States were very familiar with "The Wealth of Nations". That is one of the reasons that the founding fathers wanted the United States to have a free market economy.

In 1936, John Maynard Keynes "General Theory of Employment, Interest and Money" was published.

Keynes believed that consumption could drive production and that all the government needed to do was stimulate enough consumption and the economy would function perfectly. Keynes seemed to believe that the government could fine tune the economy the way a master mechanic could fine tune an automobile.

Libertarians and true conservatives believe that Adam Smith was correct and that John Maynard Keynes was full of fertilizer.

The policies of Democrats and liberals flow from their belief in Keynesian economic theory.

Adam Smith's economic theories are now referred to classical economics.

In 1932, Ronald Reagan received a degree in economics and sociology from Eureka College in Eureka, Illinois.

Democrats ridiculed Ronald Reagan's supply side economic policies as voodoo economics and Reaganomics when in fact Ronald Reagan was simply applying the classical economic theories he had learned in college.

Ronald Reagan was reviled by the left because he proved that classical economic policies worked meaning that Keynesian economic policies were at best irrelevant and at worst harmful.

The Laffer Curve

Politicians and voters have been ignoring the implications of the Laffer curve for far too long. The Laffer curve demonstrated that as tax rates increased they become more of a drag on the economy. The curve was named after Arthur Laffer, an economist who worked for Ronald Reagan and originated the Laffer curve. There comes a point where further tax increases will no longer increase government revenue. After that point, government revenue drops with each new tax increase. The fact that when John F. Kennedy, Ronald Reagan, and George W. Bush cut tax revenue increased should be all the proof needed to show that further tax increases will not increase revenue to the government.

If increasing revenue is all liberal politicians want to do, they would cut taxes and continue cutting taxes until the last tax cut no longer produced an increase in revenue to the government. Taxation is about more than raising revenue. It is also about controlling people. As Milton Friedman pointed out in "Capitalism and Freedom", when the government gains more control of the economy, the government gains more control over the private lives of its' citizens. The income tax is a very inefficient tax. It costs almost 50¢ cents for every dollar collected under the income tax. The Internal Revenue System is only efficient at abusing citizens of the United States. Control is what liberal Democrat politicians are all about.

It seems counterintuitive that a laissez faire capitalist economic would be more compassionate than a socialist economic system but that is the case. "The Invisible Heart" by Russell Roberts describes in detail why a laissez faire economic is more compassionate.

In a laissez faire economic system, everything is based on personal decisions.

When a person buys or sells a product, that sale is factored in to what gets produced. When a person chooses where to sell his or her labor, that sale is factored in to the labor market. Every individual economic decision is factored into what happen is the market place. The fact that everything is based on individual decisions makes the market place more personal and more compassionate.

In a socialist or communist economic system, decisions are made by bureaucrats.

In most cases bureaucrats are making decisions for

thousands of people and sometimes millions of people. That makes the socialist and communist economic systems very impersonal and very uncompassionate.

If the government became so large that every person working in the private sector was supporting one bureaucrat, then big government would be very personal. The bureaucrat would tell the person working in the private sector what time to get up in the morning, what to eat for breakfast, what time to arrive at work, what to pack for lunch, what time to come home at night, what to eat for supper and what time to go to bed. It would be like a traditional marriage before two parent incomes became necessary. The difference is that the person working in the private sector would get no physical pleasure from the bureaucrat and the bureaucrat would do no cooking or cleaning.

If people paid more attention to the implications of the Laffer curve, it would be more difficult for Democrat politicians to convince people that tax increases are beneficial to anyone but the Stalinists who want total control over the lives of the citizens of the United States.

Sinister Pigs

Sinister pig is the name French farmers give to the boss pig that attacks other pigs attempting to take a bite from the trough.

"Sinister Pig" is also the name of a novel by Tony Hillerman. In this novel, the sinister pig is a human who acts like his namesake. His avariciousness and greed know no bounds.

Most of the problems in the world today are caused by sinister pigs.

The world's biggest sinister pigs are the international bankers who run the Federal Reserve System. The founding fathers did not want this country to have a central bank and they warned that if a central bank was put in place, the central bankers and corporate elite would rob the citizens of this country of all their wealth.

On June 16' 2010 Fortune magazine reported:

"BP ended weeks of speculation Wednesday by canceling its quarterly dividend for the rest of this year.

Chairman Carl-Henric Svanberg said the London-based oil giant made the decision after a White House Summit with President Obama."

What really happened? The sinister pigs are taking money from the middle class and giving it to the government.

The people who control BP are tied to the international bankers and corporate elite who pull Barack Obama's strings.

Before he died, George Carlin did a routine about the American dream. He said it is called the American dream because you have to be asleep to believe it.

The following quote is from alternet.org:

"He starts out slamming America's education system and moves on to how the corporations and business interests have Americans "by the ba***." Carlin says the people that run this country want nothing more than "obedient workers" and now they want our social security money and retirement. "It's a big club and you and I aren't in it," says Carlin."

BP's stockholders are paying for the oil spill caused by BP and exacerbated by government inactivity.

As usual politicians, international bankers and the corporate elite are paying nothing. That is because they are all members of the big club that George Carlin talked about.

Now that the sinister pigs have managed to steal dividends from BP stockholders, what will they go after next?

It may be just a coincidence, but one week after I finished reading "Sinister Pig", newspapers published a picture of Hillary Clinton bending over in front of a coffee machine.

Simplicity

In designing a machine, engineers try to keep the design as simple as possible because more moving parts means more things can go wrong with the machine. This principle is true not just with machines but within almost everything else in life.

Golfers try to develop a repeatable swing that causes the golf ball to fly in the same pattern every time. The simpler the swing the fewer moving parts it has and the easier it is to repeat.

Richard Marcinko, author and former military leader, says, "It's the simple plans that work."

It seems that in every area of life simplicity is an asset. Most women look great in a simple black dress. Men look elegant in a grey suit with a white shirt and striped tie. If a man wears a multi-colored plaid suit, he risks looking like a clown.

In economics, it is also the simple plans that work.

Ronald Reagan understood that it was the simple plans that worked because when he received a bachelor's degree in economics and sociology classical economic theory was what colleges taught. Classical economic theory taught that an activist government could do no possible good. Ronald Reagan graduated from Eureka College in 1932.

The theories of John Maynard Keynes did not catch on until after 1933. By the 1950's Keynesian economic theory became the dominant economic theory taught in colleges. Keynesian economic theory taught that government could fine tune an economy the way a master mechanic could fine tune an automobile. If that were true the Soviet Union would have had a booming economy.

What works in economics is freedom. Lower taxes and fewer regulations both cause economic growth. Big government which means higher taxes and more regulation is what doesn't work.

Democrats called Ronald Reagan's economic policies "voodoo economics" and "Reaganomics". It was really just classical economic theory. Ronald Reagan understood the concept of KISS (Keep it simple stupid). That is what classical economic theory teaches.

Right vs. Left

What is the real difference between the left and right in the political arena? Certainly, there is a large philosophical difference. People on the left believe that big government is the answer to every problem. People on the right of the political spectrum believe that citizens are better off with a free market economic system.

Because of this difference of opinion, leftists call those on the right heartless, cruel and worse. This noise masks the real difference between left and right.

All wealth is created in the private sector. As the government increases in size, it must confiscate more of what is produced in the private sector to support this government expansion. Less money in the private sector means that the Gross Domestic Product expands at a slower rate. If the government confiscates too much money, the economy stops growing and it may even decline in size.

The world has known two extremes in economic and political systems. One extreme is the constitutionally limited republic with a laissez-faire capitalist economic system that the founding fathers gave this country. This system gives political freedom, personal freedom, and economic freedom. It leads to prosperity. The other extreme is a socialist political system with a socialist economic system. (Communism is the most virulent form of socialism.) The socialist system gives little or no economic freedom. It also limits political freedom and personal freedom. This system leads to poverty.

In 1994, Democrats made hay by calling Republicans extremists. If Republicans had responded by explaining the historic extremes in government, Republicans could have said: Yes, we are extremists for freedom and democrats are socialist extremists. At the time, I was baffled to see Republicans pass up that golden opportunity. (Of course, if Republicans had capitalized on that opportunity, it might have forced them to put their money where their mouths were. In fact, the thinking of so-called conservative politicians, today, reminds me of the way Ambrose Bierce translated "Cogito ergo sum.": "I think that I think therefore I think that I am.")

Smaller government that confiscates less wealth from the private sector leads to more rapid expansion of the economy. Over several years a smaller government means a much larger Gross Domestic Product.

Business owners know that if an item has a fixed cost of $5, they will make more money selling 20 items for $6 each rather than selling 1 item for $10. The same principle holds true for tax rates. If the government takes a smaller percentage of company profits, those companies can produce more goods and services and they can hire more employees and pay those employees higher wages. If the government takes a smaller percentage of individuals' wages, those individuals can purchase more goods and services. This increased economic activity leads to more government revenue at lower tax rates. Conversely, higher tax rates lead to fewer jobs, lower wages and higher prices.

Leftist policies always require big government. That is why socialist and communist countries are always mired in poverty.

What has happened in Michigan since a leftist became governor? Michigan's economy has become stagnant. Jennifer Granholm's leftist policies continue to cause Michigan companies to leave the state along with Michigan jobs and Michigan residents. The Gulf Coast had Katrina; we have Jennifer.

Nullification

The following sentence is one of the Wikipedia definitions of nullification.

- Nullification (U.S. Constitution), a legal theory that a U.S. State has the right to nullify, or invalidate, any federal law which that state has deemed unconstitutional.

Several states are considering passing nullification laws in regard to legislation being passed by the current congress and signed by the current president.

The following two paragraphs are from the Uncommon Sense blog.

"If the federal government passes a law that is unconstitutional a state legislature writes a resolution, passes it, then sends it to the be signed by the governor telling the federal government that the law does not exist in that state. This is well within the states duties and rights.

Currently, as many as twenty five states are considering nullification tactics against a wide variety of proposed federal laws such as Real ID, gun control and health care reform. This is the answer for turning back the final health care bill that is ultimately coming."

"Nullification: How to Resist Federal Tyranny in the 21st Century" by Thomas E. Woods Jr. is being touted, by conservative talk show hosts, as a great book and a game plan to defeat the leftists currently running Washington.

Nullification may be just the platform conservative candidates need to show voters that they have a plausible plan of action to reclaim the freedoms being stolen from them by tyrannical politicians.

The Law That Never Was

The following is a quote from Bill Benson's web page: "The authority of the federal government to collect its income tax depends upon the 16th Amendment to the U.S. Constitution, the federal income tax amendment, which was allegedly ratified in 1913. After a year of extensive research, <u>Bill Benson</u> discovered that the 16th Amendment was not ratified by the required 3/4 of the states, but nevertheless Secretary of State Philander Knox fraudulently announced ratification."

On January 10, 2008, the Federal District Court in Chicago issued a permanent injunction against Bill Benson on the grounds that he was falsely telling people that the 16th amendment was never ratified.

How can a court issue an injunction that prevents a person from expressing his opinion without violating the 1st amendment?

According to Bill Benson, the court refused to look at the evidence that the 16th amendment was never ratified.

By the end of 1984, Bill Benson had visited every state capitol in the country. According to Mr. Benson's research not one state legally ratified the 16th amendment.

If what Bill Benson is saying is not true, why is the government so fearful of the American people hearing what he has to say?

In 1913, Woodrow Wilson's administration started the United States on the progressive path.

Progressives believe in big government controlling the lives of the citizens. They believe in politicians ruling like kings or emperors.

Ceteris Paribus

The following paragraph is from Wikipedia.

*"**Ceteris Paribus** or **caeteris paribus** is a <u>Latin</u> phrase, literally translated as "with other things the same," or "all other things being equal or held constant." It is an example of an <u>ablative absolute</u> and is commonly rendered in English as "all other things being equal." A prediction, or a statement about <u>causal</u> or logical connections between two states of affairs, is qualified by *ceteris paribus* in order to acknowledge, and to rule out, the possibility of other factors that could override the relationship between the <u>antecedent</u> and the <u>consequent</u>."*

Ceteris paribus is one of the favorite phrases of liberal economists.

Liberal economist might say, "Ceteris paribus, a tax increase of 10% will increase state revenue by 2 billion dollars."

What that economist is really saying is that if the increase in taxes has no effect on the actions of buyers and sellers, then the government will get the predicted revenue increase.

Liberal economists are famous for their failed predictions but they almost always cover themselves by saying "ceteris paribus".

Paul R. Ehrlich is a great example of a liberal economist whose predictions always miss the mark.

None of the catastrophes predicted in his book "The Population Bomb" have come to pass.

Paul R. Ehrlich's favorite phrase should be "ceteris paribus" and it probably is.

The solution to all of this country's problems is simply to get big government out of the way. The U.S. economy could rebound in less than one year.

Not being a liberal, I didn't need to use the phrase "ceteris paribus".

Government Intervention

What happens when the government subsidizes an activity? That activity increases.

Lyndon Johnson claimed that there was an epidemic of illegitimate births in the United States. In order to solve that problem, the federal government started subsidizing giving birth to illegitimate children. After that, the number of illegitimate births in the United States skyrocketed.

On June 2, 2000 Ben Boychuk and Matthew Robinson wrote in the Washington Times: "Since the 1960s we've learned that the Great Society was an extended war on the role of the father in bringing up children. Let's not make the sanctimonious phrase, "quality education daycare" a synonym for a war against mom."

Before the government introduced third party payers into the health care system, doctors and hospitals had to keep costs low enough that patients could pay out of pocket. Paying, out of pocket, encouraged patients to spend less time at the doctor's office.

There is an obvious pattern here. When progressives want to expand the size of government, they claim there is a crisis and only the government can solve the problem. The government solution creates a much bigger problem than the one that existed previously. Progressives point at the government created problem and say that only the government can solve this bigger problem.

The real solution is to keep the government out of the loop.

The Council on Foreign Relations

The following paragraphs are from a term paper by William Blase titled "The Council on Foreign Relations (CFR) and The New World Order.

" If one group is effectively in control of national governments and multinational corporations; promotes world government through control of media, foundation grants, and education; and controls and guides the issues of the day; then they control most options available. The Council on Foreign Relations (CFR), and the financial powers behind it, have done all these things, and promote the "New World Order", as they have for over seventy years."

"James Warburg, son of CFR founder Paul Warburg, and a member of FDR's "brain trust," testified before the Senate Foreign Relations Committee on February 17, 1950, "We shall have world government whether or not you like it--by conquest or consent.""

In "Arguing with Idiots" Glenn Beck uses the following quote from former CFR chairman David Rockefeller: "Some believe we are part of a secret cabal working against the best interests of the United States, characterizing my family and me as "internationalists" and of conspiring with others around the world to build a more integrated global political and economic structure-one world, if you will. If that's the charge, I stand guilty and I am proud of it."

Does anyone need more proof that there is a conspiracy to push the United States into a one world government?

Who would gain the most by have a one world government in place? The elites like Rockefeller's, the Bush's, the Rothschild's, and all the other rich families in the world. Everyone else would be their peons.

Deficit Spending

What is deficit spending? In regard to government, it means spending more than is received in tax revenue.

What is wrong with deficit spending? Deficit spending, by the federal government, leads directly to inflation which is a hidden tax meaning that the dollar buys less in goods and services because the government has already spend a portion of that dollar.

Conservative economists favor laws requiring all levels of government to have a balanced budget because that forces the government to balance spending and tax revenue. Most politicians do not favor laws requiring balanced budgets because raising taxes in order to increase spending causes more public scrutiny of political activity.

In the "The Devil's Dictionary", published in 1911,

Ambrose Bierce defined arena as: "In politics, an imaginary rat-pit in which the statesman wrestles with his record." The more light there is on political activity, the more wrestling politicians have to do with their records. A balanced budget requirement causes more public scrutiny than most politicians want to deal with.

Let's look at what has happened to the value of the dollar since the Federal Reserve System was put in place in 1913. According to the League of the Scarlet Pimpernel by October 19, 2007, the dollar had lost 96% of its value.

Who does inflation hurt the most? People on fixed incomes suffer the most because they are not in a position to increase their income. That group includes the elderly and most of the poor.

The fact that the Federal Reserve System can print money out of thin air allows politicians to spend as much as they like.

What difference would a gold standard make?

Harry Browne

Who was Harry Browne? Harry Browne was the author of 19 books, thousands of articles and a radio talk show host. He ran for president on the Libertarian ticket in 1996 and 2000.

One of Harry Browne's greatest contributions to this country was a book that explains how the United States went from a constitutionally limited Republic with freedom for all its citizens to fascist state.

"Why Government Doesn't Work" by Harry Browne explains why the United States is where it is today.

The following is a brief synopsis of "Why Government Doesn't Work":

This book demonstrates persuasively why government programs:

- Have a failure rate over 99%,
- Never live up to their promises,
- Too often do the exact *opposite* of what was promised for them,
- Always cost far more than their initial estimates, and
- Create the conditions that justify enlarging themselves and adding more government programs.

The book provides answers to numerous questions that are sometimes perplexing:

- Why so many people keep falling for political promises,
- How America went from the land of the free to the land of government dominance,
- Why new government intrusions always wind up hurting the innocent more than the guilty, and
- How to get people to give up their favorite government programs.

Unfortunately, even when he was running for president, most people did not know who Harry Browne was. Fortunately, some of the people who have read "Why Government doesn't Work" have been bringing it to the attention of people on the internet.

Anyone who reads "Why Government Doesn't Work" will understand why the American people are no longer free and what needs to be done to regain freedom.

Progressives

Progressives always portray themselves as champions of the underdog especially black and other minority group members.

What progressives actually do is a far cry from what they claim to do.

The following was copied from Wikipedia:

"In 1912, "an unprecedented number" of African Americans left the Republican Party to cast their vote for Democrat Wilson. They were encouraged by his promises of support for their issues. The issue of segregation came up early in his presidency when, at an April 1913 cabinet meeting, Albert Burleson, Wilson's Postmaster General, complained about working conditions at the Railway Mail Service. Offices and restrooms became segregated, sometimes by partitions erected between seating for white and African-American employees in Post Office Department offices, lunch rooms, and bathrooms, as well as in the <u>Treasury</u> and the <u>Bureau of Engraving and Printing</u>. It also became accepted policy for "Negro" employees of the Postal Service to be reduced in rank or dismissed. And unlike his predecessors <u>Grover Cleveland</u> and <u>Theodore Roosevelt</u>, Wilson accommodated Southern opposition to the re-appointment of an African American to the position of <u>Register of the Treasury</u> and other positions within the federal government. This set the tone for Wilson's attitude to race throughout his presidency, in which the rights of African Americans were sacrificed, for what he felt would be the more important longer term progress of the common good."

Like Woodrow Wilson, Lyndon Baines Johnson promised minorities great benefits from the federal government. What did LBJ really think of minorities?

"I'll have those n*ggers voting Democratic for the next 200 years." — Lyndon B. Johnson to two governors on Air Force One according to Ronald Kessler's Book, "**Inside The White House**".

The real goal of all progressives is to make as many people as possible dependent on government. So far they have had more success in the black community than in the white community. By making more blacks than whites dependent on the government they have done far more damage to the black community than the white community.

Progressives have all of us in their sights. Who will they

get next?

www.ingramcontent.com/pod-product-compliance
Lightning Source LLC
Chambersburg PA
CBHW060906280326
41934CB00007B/1210